A Living Society

A Living Society

Jonathan Mantle

JAMES
JAMES

CONTENTS

1 Looking Ahead in the Oldest Town   7

2 A Community within the Community   16

3 The Intricacies of Modern Business   25

4 The Challenges of Change   35

5 Co-operation and Competition   49

6 Recession and Recovery   55

7 A Tradition of Trade   63

8 Your Society: Looking Ahead   68

   Index   72

ISBN 0 907383 181

Designed by Eleanor Hayes
Photographic Acknowledgements: Paul Barker, Bob Cross,
Tony Ellis, Tony Nichols and Van-Cols of Colchester Ltd.

Printed by G. Canale Co., Italy

Published by James & James (Publishers) Limited
Gordon House Business Centre
6 Lissenden Gardens
London NW5 1LX

FOREWORD

Our Society approaches the new millennium with confidence and from a position of strength. As such, we should take the time to proudly reflect on the achievements of those who came before us.

However, we must continue to embrace change and concentrate all our efforts and resources on addressing the challenges of the future. The principles and ideals on which our Society was founded are as appropriate today as they were in 1861, but it is incumbant on us all to interpret them in a manner relevant to society in the twenty-first century.

Chris Blanchett
Chief Executive Officer

1

Facing page: Colchester Castle. The magnificent Norman keep stands at the centre of the town.

LOOKING AHEAD
IN THE
OLDEST TOWN

Some 140 years ago a small group of people met in a coffee room in Colchester to discuss a new enterprise. Led by John Castle, a silk weaver, and his friend, a Mr Dand (history does not record the latter's Christian name), they founded the 'Colchester and East Essex Co-operative and Industrial Society'. Run on a part-time basis from a small back room, it was a humble beginning for what was to be the fulfilment of an ambitious vision.

This is the story of how it grew to become the largest and most distinctive retail chain in the region. Owned entirely by its 150,000 members, who share in its profits through an annual dividend, and employing approximately 2,000 people, it owns over eighty trading outlets servicing an area of 600 square miles.

In addition to the commercial operation, it supports cultural, social and sporting activities throughout the region. Its mission in the community is not at odds with – indeed, it enhances – its central purpose as a successful business in a highly competitive consumer market. As such it is one of an elite group of independent Co-operative societies. But to revert to the beginning...

In 1861 Colchester, renowned as Britain's oldest recorded town, was characterised by its independence of mind, possibly reinforced by its relative isolation – the railway arrived only in 1843. A market town in an essentially rural area, it was perhaps less obviously affected by the Victorian technical and industrial advances which were making a huge impact on the rapidly growing industrial cities. But its ordinary working people did share with their compatriots in the rest of the country a life of hardship unimaginable today. Even skilled artisans like Castle and Dand had few rights and fewer expectations, and fought a daily battle to support their families.

A precarious existence was made worse by unscrupulous

John Castle, the founder of the Society in 1861.

Notice calling to form a society in 1861.

Notice is hereby given, that a Meeting will be held at Mr J. Martins — opposite the Hythe Church — on Monday Eve next at 7 o'Clock. for the purpose of forming a Co-operative Society. the Rules, and Regulations, of which will be fully explained to those who feel disposed to attend.

shopkeepers. As Castle wrote in his memoirs: 'Some of the bakers were selling what they represented to be a 4lb loaf, but which I proved more than once only weighed 3lb 10oz.'

Many working people saw little hope of improving their lot, and some even resented the efforts of others to do so: 'They did not seem to appreciate what anyone might do for their good,' Castle wrote, 'especially if they saw anyone advance themselves above them in the social scale.' Others, like Castle and Dand, were convinced that poverty and hardship were not only unjust, but unnecessary in a democratic society, and that a solution was at hand. Early in 1861, they called a meeting 'of about 12 respectable men' at Thompson's Coffee Room in Short Wyre Street, where, according to Castle, 'We discussed the desirability of a Co-operative Society in Colchester.'

Co-operative Societies were relatively new, being established to enable workers to trade with other workers and secure basic provisions of good quality at a fair price. It had first been put into practice in Rochdale, in 1844, where a group of twenty-eight people contributed £1 apiece to buy bulk supplies, reselling to individual members, and dividing profits to each member according to his or her purchases.

At the end of their first meeting, Castle and his friends resolved to send to the Rochdale Society for a copy of its rules. Subsequently they mustered twenty-eight members at a joining fee of 1s. each, raised their first capital, and elected a committee. By 9 August 1861, *Essex Standard and Eastern Counties Advertiser* was able to report the

Flour was the first product that the Society sold in the early days.

foundation of the 'Colchester and East Essex Co-operative and Industrial Society ['Industrial' remained formally part of the name until it was dropped in the 1960s] . . . for supplying the members with provisions and other articles of prime necessity at cost prices, or as near cost prices as the necessary expenses of a simple and inexpensive machinery of business will allow.'

The report went on:

> The Colchester Society at present numbers fifty members, most of them, we understand, from the respectable artisan class, who have engaged the room in Culver Street, lately occupied by the working men's club. We are informed that for the present the Co-operative Society intend to open their store for the sale of bread and flour only, and that on three days in the week. The extension of their trading will depend upon the success attending this first movement.

Despite limited opening hours and meagre premises, the success of the Society was immediate: 'We bought a sack of flour, borrowed scales and weights – I lent a basin which answered for a flour scoop,' Castle recalled. 'Thus we started in a small business, which was destined to grow very fast.' The first fifty members and customers were working men like Castle, many in skilled trades: baker, engineer, provision dealer, bootmaker, bookseller and suchlike. Some were active in local politics and trade unionism, while others were budding entrepreneurs; all were united in the common goal of co-operation. In line with Co-operative principles, and in return for their custom, which in the first week amounted to the considerable sum of £5, the Society periodically returned its profits to members in the form of a dividend calculated on the value of their purchases; anticipating by well over a century the supposedly modern invention of the 'loyalty card'.

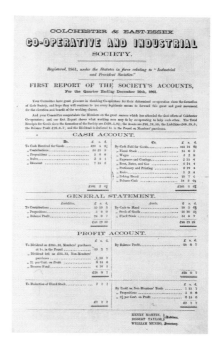

The Society's first company accounts, 1861.

The corner of Long Wyre Street and Culver Street in 1854.

Another early product of the Society was Co-operative Tea, bought from the Co-operative Wholesale Society. This advertisement, probably from the 1900s, reflects how widespread the movement had become.

The continuation of this early success depended to a large extent on the voluntary unpaid support of members in the day-to-day operations of the Society. They worked long hours in their day jobs, and yet made time to serve on the Committee in the evenings. They felt themselves to be an extended family and acted as such. When their first full-time shopman, James Nevard, was suddenly taken ill and died of a fever, the Committee voted to provide his widow with financial support and even today the Society provides a death-in-service benefit. By this time, in 1862, many more members had joined, and the shop had grown from a single room to eight rooms, a butcher's shop and slaughterhouse in the former Blomfield's Butchery, still in Culver Street, at the rear of St Nicholas Church. The Society first rented and then bought these premises, which required extensive renovation. John Castle, by this time purchaser and treasurer, was meanwhile having problems with finding shopmen of the calibre of the late and lamented Mr Nevard: 'While our new building was going on,' he recalled, 'we came to a very large deficiency in profits, and I acted as a detective and traced two of our shopmen to houses of ill fame, so that they had to leave us.' The Board Minutes for 1864 record: 'Proposed and seconded that Mr Castle sleep on the premises during the building of the stores.'

The principles of Co-operation as laid down in the rules included a commitment to nourish the minds as well as the bodies of members (universal education had yet to be introduced). This was put into practice by the formation of the Education Committee, which initiated the involvement of the Society in the community and, as we shall see, continues in numerous forms to this day. The new building, with its expanded shop, greater range of foodstuffs and drapery department, accordingly included assembly rooms and a reading room. The latter offered four daily papers including *The Times*, with

The changing face of Long Wyre Street from the late nineteenth century (*right*) to the present day (*facing page*).

Manningtree Co-operative Society, opened in 1907 and was one of many Co-operatives absorbed by the Colchester Society.

twelve weeklies and five monthlies available in the evenings for members; this was at a time when no such facilities existed for the benefit of the general public; the service continued until 1955. The library contained eighty volumes donated by John Taylor, owner and landlord of the first premises of the Society and proprietor of the *Essex Standard.* 'Penny Readings' and concerts also took place here. In October 1867, the new premises were opened by the Mayor of Colchester and 500 members sat down to a celebratory tea. Afterwards they adjourned to the Town Hall where they were gratified to hear that with the growth of both the membership and average individual expenditure, annual sales of the Society of the 28 shilling enterprise founded sixteen years before had increased to no less than £7,000.

Throughout the rest of the nineteenth century, and into the twentieth, the Society and the town of Colchester grew and prospered. Contrary to the Co-op movement's later image, the Colchester society was anything but old-fashioned in its outlook. When a trading crisis arose in 1873 owing to losses in the bakery and drapery departments, there were resignations, and the restoration of confidence was aided by the decision to use the reserve fund to maintain the dividend – and the trust – of the membership. Today's talk of corporate governance implies this is a modern invention; yet a strong sense of accountability existed at many levels throughout the Society from the beginning. In 1874, for example, the Society placed its first order for coal with the Co-operative Wholesale Society (CWS), but only on condition that the Committee paid for and tested the consignment personally before supplying it to members. Within the wider Co-operative movement, the Society was already acquiring greater prominence. In 1875, the Society hosted the first congress of Eastern Region societies, and was represented for the first time at the Co-operative Congress in London. The growth of the business mirrored that of Colchester town. In 1878, the Society purchased a shop in Long Wyre Street and fitted it out to sell boots and drapery. In the same year, with the development of the Colchester New Town estate increasing the population, the Society was quick to alter its rules to enable it to buy up land and build houses to be sold to members. On the same site it built a new bakery of the most advanced type. One night the Committee made a surprise visit to inspect the premises. When they arrived they discovered that their pride and joy, instead of humming with baking activity, was locked up and in darkness. The head baker was fired and his assistant appointed in his place. John Castle, the founder of the Society and former manager of the Culver Street store, was persuaded to become full-time manager of the bakery on a wage of 24s. for a seventy-hour week.

The new bakery was followed by a string of openings in and around Colchester over the next few years. These began in 1885 with the grandly titled 'Branch Number 1' grocery in Colchester New Town. Pessimists on the Committee shook their heads and declared that sales in Culver Street would suffer as a result. In the event, the new shop was immediately successful while sales of the first were unaffected. Thus inspired, the Committee voted in the same year to buy a block of buildings in North Station Road and convert these into a grocery and bakery. At the request of members, more branches followed: butcheries in Kendall Road, North Station Road; confectionery and hardware shops opened in Wyre Street; coal depots opened at St Botolph's and Hythe stations. The Society bought a farm, Whitehose, at West Bergholt, and opened its own house mortgage department. By 1895, the administrative role of secretary was proving too demanding for the current incumbent, R. J. Burrell, to perform in his spare time, and the Committee appointed Robert Bultitude as the first full-time secretary, a position he would

The corner of Long Wyre Street and Culver Street in 1874. Colchester Co-operative Society occupied the building on the right.

Statue of Queen Victoria at Marine Parade in Dovercourt.

Mistley (*facing page*) and neighbouring Manningtree were flourishing quays on the River Stour until the end of the nineteenth cenury. Co-op shops in Manningtree continue to service the area today.

The seaside town of Dovercourt was one of the earlier Co-op locations.

hold for thirty-seven years. By 1903, when the Society opened a central butchery in Long Wyre Street, there were 6,300 members and sales had reached £130,000 a year.

These openings, whether they were of a banana-ripening room or the Society's first abattoir, were invariably attended by large numbers of members and marked by speeches applauding the virtues of the Co-operative movement. As the Society reached its jubilee year in 1911, the Board of Management and members had much to celebrate. From tiny resources, and in the face of hostility from local shopkeepers, they had built a benevolent trading empire with nearly 8,000 members and annual sales of £164,000 capable of meeting, virtually at cost price, an ever-widening range of needs of the customer, to whom they then returned the profits. The Society had expanded from Colchester into the towns and villages of East Essex, opening 'country' branches in Lexden, Wivenhoe, Rowhedge and Manningtree, with more, like Brightlingsea, shortly to follow. It had a fleet of twenty-seven horse-drawn vans and a Dennis 30-cwt petrol van at its disposal, which was deployed over this growing area for home deliveries. It had a thriving Education Committee and Women's Guild, both of which were active locally and affiliated to the Co-operative movement at national level. The members of the Board of Management were respected as leading lights in civic life, in which many of them would also play roles as justices of the peace, alderman and mayor. They were more than merely the sum of their parts; they were a community within the community. The coming years of war, peace, the Depression and war, were to see this community demonstrate its strengths through good and bad times alike.

2

A COMMUNITY WITHIN THE COMMUNITY

The names of members on war memorials across Colchester and East Essex are sad evidence of the substantial size and geographical spread of the Society by the beginning of the First World War. In the immediate aftermath of the outbreak of hostilities, it was business as usual. Steelwork went up for the rebuilding of 'Colco Corner' in Wyre Street as a three-storey flagship store for the Society; completion, however, would be delayed for the duration. The membership continued to grow towards 10,000, and the increase in sales contributed to a healthy dividend and solid reserves. Two of the Society's horses and carts were commandeered by the Army; the rest of the transport fleet, manned by staff and members of the Society, voluntarily carried wounded troops from St

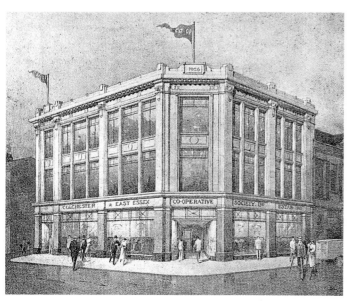

'Colco Corner' completed in 1926 still houses a part of the Co-op department store.

Botolph's station to the Military Hospital. The billeting of troops in private houses increased sales. However, it was not long before the effects of the wartime economy began to bite. Trade with non-members was discontinued, except for members of the armed forces. The butcheries at Manningtree and Brightlingsea were forced to close through lack of staff. In 1917, the Society adopted the collective life assurance scheme for members in conjunction with the Co-operative Insurance Society; this was at no cost to members, and individual claims were paid on production of a death certificate and in proportion to the size of the deceased member's purchases. In the same year, as the result of a Government Order that bread could no longer be sold under twelve hours old, some of the Society's premises were converted into a bread store. No new customers were accepted for coal.

The Baker's float at the Colchester carnival in the mid-1920s. Horse-drawn carriages were typically used for the transport of goods.

By 1921, the Depression was biting more deeply in economic terms than the war, and staff took a pay cut of 5 per cent. In the same year, however, in response to local demand, the Society opened a new branch for 'country' members at Mersea. Other smaller societies were feeling the pressure more acutely, and could no longer cope on their own; the Co-operative ethos included an obligation to offer help in these cases, and for this reason Colchester and East Essex Society absorbed the Tiptree 'Self-Help' Society, taking on its trade and membership.

Colchester and East Essex Society's newspaper *The Wheatsheaf* gives vivid glimpses of the lives of its members in these years, and of how many areas of their lives the Society reached. These ranged from shopping to finance, funerals, education and politics: a comprehensive service in the department store of life, from the cradle to the grave. Nothing was too much trouble, as *The Wheatsheaf* of February 1922, indicated: 'We are glad our Tiptree friends are supporting their own store. We would remind them that we will do all in our power to assist them in any way. If the manager (Mr F. Blunt) has not got in stock any article you require, well, he can soon 'phone for it, and we assure you it shall be sent over smartly. Let us have all your trade; we know we can serve you well.'

To the membership in general, the editorial staff of *The Wheatsheaf* issued stirring rallying cries which may seem naïve in the climate of today, reading as they do like exhortations to members to shop their way to the workers' paradise. At the time, however, its editorial comment was a fair reflection of the way many people felt in a so-called 'land fit for heroes'. It also provided a significant insight into an insecure and frightening time. As *The Wheatsheaf* declared in January 1922:

A prize-winning butcher's shop in the 1920s.

A window display at a grocery store in Witham for the 1931 Co-op Window Display Competition.

Unemployment, short time, and the disturbances of industry generally, due in great part to the aftermath of war, have been with us, and we have been powerless to avert the tragedy that has followed. We have seen, in our streets, ill-clad and semi-starved children and broken-hearted, weary women, tired of the seemingly unequal battle of life.

And all this time you have a movement which, if you would only give it all your support, would do much to alter the whole trend of economic events. You may have been waiting for a prophet to arise to lead us into a better land, but all the time you could have been helping to make that better state.

Have you ever thought seriously of co-operation – what it stands for and what it could accomplish? I am afraid you are rather apt to look upon the stores as a kind of dividend-making machine, a place where you think you pay a little more for your goods and then get the surplus returned at the end of each half year; but our movement is something far more than that. Our aim is the setting up of a co-operative commonwealth wherein there will be no men struggling for the work they cannot get, no sad-eyed worried mothers and no half-starved children; where there shall be equal opportunity for all, and where life will be truly joyous.

That is the work we are endeavouring to do, and we want your help. I tell you we are beginning to be a power in the land, and our enemies begin to fear us; but by your unswerving loyalty and your united endeavour we shall win through and found that commonwealth in which man will live the life that is really worth living.

Co-operation and political idealism were synonymous among the management and employees of the Society. By 1926, it was a condition of service that all members of staff should be current members

An advertisement from the Society to assist members to buy their own homes from 1924.

of their respective trade unions. The Co-operative movement as a whole was closely involved in Labour politics; individual societies sponsored Co-operative Labour Party Members of Parliament, and some do so to this day.

The Depression heightened political awareness in members and prompted innovation in the retail operations. Colchester and East Essex Society broke with the tradition of exclusively cash trading, introducing credit trading and hire purchase, still with the dividend payable, to enable hard-pressed members to make larger purchases such as household goods, furniture, boots, clothes and hardware. These products included an increasing number manufactured by the Co-operative Wholesale Society 'in your own factory'; many manufacturers would not supply Co-operatives, which they saw as undercutting private retailers whose prices had to be high enough to pay profits to conventional shareholders. In addition to a wide range of foodstuffs, clothes and boots and shoes, products manufactured in-house included perambulators, children's scooters, bicycles and the 'Defiant' radio, the latter named in response to the boycotting of manufacturers. Shoppers in Colchester and East Essex were appreciative of the quality and value for money these products represented in these hard times. When the new 'Colco Corner' boots and clothing store eventually opened for business in Wyre Street, unemployment was so great that there were 191 applications for the post of caretaker.

Throughout the Depression, and helped by innovations such as credit trading and hire purchase, the Society and its members continued to grow, with nearly 17,000 members and sales of over £500,000 a year by 1926. The Society had 400 staff, including its own

A 1929 edition of the *Colco Sales Bulletin* advertising everything from clothes and shoes to galvanised baths, bicycles and hardware repairs.

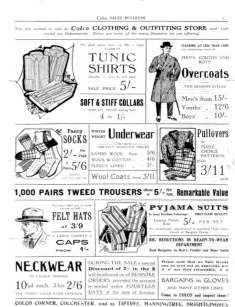

Interior of a hardware shop in Witham, *circa* 1920s.

building works department, which fitted out its new shops, bakeries and dairies; it also held the deeds for house property on mortgage to the value of £100,000. The Transport Department's thirty-six horse-drawn vans and sixteen motor vehicles delivered a wide range of goods across Colchester and East Essex according to schedules regularly updated in *The Wheatsheaf.* The Transport Committee announced that members could recharge their car batteries at the Society's Garage in Military Road, Colchester, for a modest fee. The range and quality of services grew, with pasteurised bottled milk being introduced in 1928 at the model dairy in Wimpole Road, replacing the traditional method of serving and measuring milk from an open can on the customer's doorstep. A funeral parlour opened in Winsley Road in 1932; an optical service in Victoria Place in the same year; and a pharmacy in Long Wyre Street in 1935. The *Colco Sales Bulletin* kept members informed about upcoming bargains and helped them shop their way through the Depression, with special offers on everything from galvanised baths to felt hats, children's socks and tea sets.

Not only by its retailing policy, but also with its programmes of lectures, concerts, readings, sports days, educational courses and children's activities, the Society and its values were a very real presence in the lives of many thousands of members and the families of its employees: 'The Society was a family,' recalled Dennis Dallender, who later became its president, 'and everyone knew everyone else. The dividend meant a lot to people in those days; it would pay for the children's shoes. Many working people gained a lot of education through association with the Co-operative movement; it taught them to look after themselves better and take greater responsibility for their lives.' Dorothy Dallender worked as a cashier and in the footwear department, and was equally involved in the movement: 'We lived Co-op,' she recalled.

The introduction of bottled pasteurised milk completely changed the way milk was stored and sold.

Dallender was a young man in the grocery department of the Clacton Society, when Colchester Society took it over in 1931. His father was on the Committee of Management of the Clacton Society, and with the merger joined the Committee of Management of Colchester and East Essex, as in time would Dennis and his daughter, Dianne Dallender-Jones, who is on the board today. The Clacton Society was renamed as a branch of Colchester and East Essex Society, and subsequent investment has created the substantial range of Co-op shops and services in Clacton-on-Sea which flourishes to this day. Even with the merger, however, there was in those days a vast difference between Colchester and the rest of East Essex. With few telephones and cars, communities were self-contained. This characteristic was evident in the individual societies, which often had second and third generations of families on their staff. In spite

The milk receiving room.

of their united belief in the Co-operative movement, societies could be fiercely protective of their own territory, and dismissive of other societies, their dividends and their practices. Don Barker, like his father and his wife, worked in the Harwich Society, which was independent at the time and had every intention of staying so: 'To me, Colchester was another world,' he recalled, 'and even when we eventually did become part of Colchester Society, we were still very much one of the "country branches"'. There would be many more years of proud independence before Harwich, Dovercourt and Parkeston Society, as it became known, was taken over by Colchester and East Essex Society in 1967.

In August 1936, the seventy-fifth anniversary of the founding of the Society saw over 3,000 children of members gather on a summer day for a fête and gala at the employees' sports ground in King Harold Road, Colchester. In the twenty-five years since its jubilee, and in spite of war and the Depression, the membership had grown from nearly 8,000 to over 30,000, and annual sales from just over £34,000, to nearly £800,000. A special issue of the *Colchester Co-operative Recorder* celebrated these achievements, and gave members the latest news about the Co-operative movement around the world, such as its thriving agricultural activities in the lands of the British Empire, and its oppression under the Fascist dictatorships in Europe. It was by now clear that the regimes of Hitler and Mussolini posed a serious threat. Nevertheless, on the day of its children's tea and gala, the Society and its special edition of the newspaper were in joyful mood:

> What of the Future? The future is bright with promise. Almost every department urgently requires more accommodation. At the moment extensive stock and showrooms are being built at the rear of the Long Wyre Street shops. Land has been acquired for the erection of branches at Old Heath, Tollesbury and Holland-on-Sea . . .

Finally, should the reader not have linked up with us in this successful experiment in mutual trading, a cordial invitation is extended to him, or her, to join us at once.

This bright future, it transpired, was soon to be overshadowed by a new world war, even more devastating than the last one and with a far more drastic effect upon the lives of civilians. Shortly after the outbreak of war, food rationing was introduced, and the Society received 131,140 registrations for butter, bacon, ham and sugar. This meant that approximately half the population of Colchester would draw their supplies of these basic commodities from the Society. Men were conscripted and horses and motor vehicles were commandeered or dispersed. A benevolent fund was formed for the dependants of members of staff serving in the armed forces, subscribed by the transfer of £500 from the general fund and the donation by members of staff of one penny in the pound of their wages each week. A house was purchased in Bedford to preserve the Society's books and records, and to serve as an emergency office in the event of an evacuation of Colchester. The Society also purchased a fire engine, which members of staff were trained to operate, and appointed a full-time Air Raid Precautions Officer. The first casualties became the next names of members to be inscribed on war memorials across Colchester and East Essex.

The Society found ways to overcome the wartime restrictions on building, and so continued to grow, buying other shops and businesses in the area. These included butcheries at Tolleshunt d'Arcy, Walton-on-the-Naze, Wivenhoe and West Mersea; a jewellery business, drapery and fish shop in Colchester; another drapery and a pharmacy at Clacton-on-Sea; groceries at Dedham, Tollesbury, Walton, Clacton-on-Sea and Bures; a boot shop at Manningtree; a coal business at Coggeshall; and pharmacies at Lexden and Walton-on-the-Naze. Many of these business were already closed or closing. At the end of the war, in 1945, the Society also absorbed the

Grocery shop in Dedham today.

Dedham Vale. The Society have owned a grocery store in Dedham since the Second World War.

Above left: A pharmaceutical shop in the 1930s.

Above right: The Harwich, Dovercourt and Parkeston Co-operative Society shop during the 1920s.

Coggeshall 'Heart-in-Hand' Co-operative Society, which became its Coggeshall branches.

Even after the end of the war, trading conditions were extremely difficult, with the country as a whole virtually bankrupted by the war effort, and no end in sight to shortages and bureaucracy. From reduced sales and dividends, to restricted community activities, every aspect of the Society would be affected: 'The peace we have all been looking for for so long has come,' the Education Committee wrote in the first report and balance sheet after the war. 'The hopes we once had of going forward immediately with a full programme, however, have had to be deferred owing to circumstances and we have had to exercise some patience. However, it has been possible to arrange one or two things.'

The Society's 75th anniversary celebrations at the Co-op Hall in Colchester, 1936.

3

THE INTRICACIES OF
MODERN BUSINESS

Just before the end of the war, the famous Beveridge Report set out the guidelines for probably the most fundamental development of post-war Britain – the welfare state. Its ideas included many of the principles of the Co-operative movement. Free education and healthcare, and common ownership of key resources, were top priorities for the new Labour government which had been swept to power in the election of 1945. As keen Co-operators, many, if not most, members of the Society strongly supported these aims. However, implementing these policies involved a considerable degree of government regulation. This included continued rationing, higher taxes and increased wage scales, which both hindered trade and yet required an increase in the same, if they were not to eat into the resources of employers. As a result, paradoxically, even the Co-operative societies, while politically welcoming the change, found themselves sharing the nervousness of conventional retailers in the new business climate. The president of the Society, F. A. Pope, and his Committee wrote:

Men's clothing (*left*) and ladies' coats section (*right*) of the department store in Colchester during the late 1950s.

The St Nicholas site under development for the Society's flagship furniture store in 1955–6.

Facing page: Wivenhoe Quay. In common with almost all delightful towns in north-east Essex, Colchester Co-op has a presence in Wivenhoe.

We are not unmindful of the difficulties under which our increasing trade has been accomplished. Some 250 of our employees have returned from the Forces and have had to resume work under considerably different conditions from those which they left.

We are gratified with the efforts these employees make to rehabilitate themselves to civilian life, but feel sure that members will be tolerant of any shortcomings until these employees settle down to the intricacies of modern business.

In a world where much had changed, the management of the Society remained much the same, conducted by a lay Committee of Management of eleven people, four of whom were local councillors, one an alderman and two justices of the peace. Led by the president, the Committee was responsible for four subcommittees covering the entire day-to-day operations of the Society. It published the report and balance sheet twice a year, and presided over meetings of members four times a year. Individual committee members attended meetings of one kind or another on as many as five nights a week. The secretary, although the only full-time, paid employee among them, fulfilled a purely administrative role. The Education Committee, on which some members like Fred Humm served for over forty-two years, was regarded as a rung on the ladder towards membership of the Committee of Management, and contained a dynastic element; many sons and daughters of Committee of Management members began their own involvement in running the Society in this way. Outside the head offices in Victoria Place, in the shops, depots, dairies and bakeries across the region, forty or fifty years' service, often from second and third generations of the same family, was not uncommon.

In this 'true Co-operative spirit' as the Committee of Management put it in one of their immediate post-war reports to members, they went forth to do battle. Falling profit margins, rising costs and burgeoning bureaucracy characterised life in Colchester and East Essex,

Staff outing, 1950s.

The Members' Office in Victoria Place which offered financial services to members in the 1950s.

as they did life in much of the country throughout the late 1940s and early 1950s. The men and women of the Co-op were remarkably successful in responding to the challenge, largely through their own efforts and resourcefulness, combined with a dogged adherence to traditional Co-operative principles and a gradual easing of government restrictions. The Society circumvented higher wage costs, as well as increasing sales, by converting shops to self-service, the first of their kind in the area. It extended its fleet of mobile shops and expanded and modernised other shops. A new drapery department, in Long Wyre Street, was officially opened by the former Prime Minister's wife, Violet Attlee. The new staff journal aimed to boost morale. A fleet of Co-op vans and lorries transported goods to and fro across the region.

By 1950, with over 40,000 members, half-yearly sales had reached £1 million for the first time, and by year-end were £2 million. This latest growth in business was fuelled in part by rising prices, but the Society was still able to pay a dividend of 1s.1d. in the pound on members' purchases, which averaged £1 a week. The management were also keen to expand the Society's cultural and social activities. These depended to a great degree on the contribution of voluntary youth leaders like Dennis Dallender, Basil Smith and Donald Munson, all of whom subsequently became presidents of the Society. They and others ran summer camps and youth clubs, served on the Education Committee and attended conferences of the British Federation of Co-operative Youth.

In that year of record business, 15,000 people attended Co-operative Day celebrations in Colchester, at which the Minister for War, John Strachey, made a speech.

The following year, attendance was even greater, 'despite' the Education Committee noted, 'many counter-attractions in the town and district'. These were prophetic words, for a major shift was taking place in the economy as a whole. The years of austerity were

Below left: By the 1950s, milk carts had become motorised.
Below right: The 1961 Education Committee.

coming to an end, and the country was beginning to enjoy greater consumer choice at many levels. This was a new era which would later be summed up in the phrase of Prime Minister Harold Macmillan: 'You've never had it so good.' In the case of the Society, the sense of belonging to what had been a tightly-knit community within the community, was also being shaken up. H. H. Fisher, the president of the Society, an alderman, justice of the peace and former Mayor of Colchester, sensed this with some alarm:

> May I criticise? [he wrote in *Focus*, the staff journal, in March 1952]. I have been profoundly disquieted when from time to time it has come to my notice how little some of you spend with the Society that employs you. *Prima facie*, it is none of my business, but I do suggest loyalty is demanded of you, if we are to maintain the standing of the Society, and, in particular, as a duty to your fellow employees in other departments. Also take more interest in your own affairs – your Trade Union, Workers' Advisory Council, the *Focus*, the Sports Section, our education facilities. They only function properly through individual interest.

Mrs Violet Attlee, wife of the former Prime Minister, opens a new drapery department in Long Wyre Street in 1957.

One way in which to maintain the interest of individual members was to increase the financial benefits of membership, which the Society was enabled to do by government legislation in 1952. This allowed the maximum shareholding (minimum £1) per member to rise from £200 to £500. In 1954, when all rationing came to an end, sales rose again and the Society was also able to raise its dividend from 10*d*. back to 1*s*. in the pound.

The following year H. H. Fisher, who had first served on the Committee of Management in 1922, died suddenly, just after

Below left: Cookery demonstration at the opening of St Nicholas House.
Below right: The new 'Defiant' television on display at St Nicholas House.

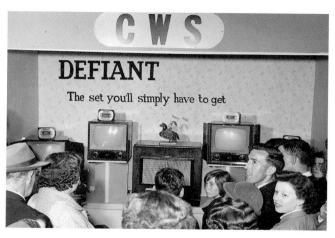

conducting a quarterly meeting of members. He was succeeded by
Dennis Dallender, who was already employed as a full-time agent
for the Co-operative Insurance Society (CIS). Dallender was steeped
in the Co-operative movement but, unlike many others who feared
change, he was also a moderniser, and his appointment brought a
quiet, but firmly progressive, style to the boardroom in Victoria
Place.

Outside the boardroom, and not far away, this modernisation was
symbolised by the development of St Nicholas House. Work began
on the site of the demolished St Nicholas Church on the corner of
St Nicholas Street and High Street in 1956. Under construction was
a flagship emporium with an exterior in the Georgian style, and an
interior incorporating the latest design ideas to show off hardware,
furnishings, electrical items, television and other goods. The

Manningtree is located on one of the many estuaries which characterise the area.

Society's existing shops in Long Wyre Street were also rebuilt, in this case by the Society's works department.

The climax of development in this period, in 1957, was the grand opening of St Nicholas House by Viscount Alexander of Hillsborough, followed in 1958 by the opening of the rebuilt Wyre Street shops and the general expansion of head office and various departments of the Society. Expansion continued in many areas during these years. Grocery and butchery shops at Monkwick, and a food hall at Shrub End, opened in 1956; in 1957, a general store and pharmacy opened at Walton-on-the-Naze; and, in 1958, a retail garage and petrol station opened in Wimpole Road, Colchester.

During these years, the community activities of the Society also grew and flourished, with the Education Department leaving its premises of over seventy years in Lion Walk, for new

The Public Service Station in Wimpole Road, Colchester, offered a complete service for motorists.

Contemporary 1920s' advertisement for Co-op products.

accommodation in New Town Road. The emphasis in the community was still firmly on self-improvement, but there was a greater appeal to consumer choice, with children's ballet, elocution and keep-fit classes among the new activities on offer.

In 1958, the Co-operative Independent Commission published a report which made various recommendations for the way forward for Britain's Co-operative Societies. It concluded that societies should sell their goods at the market prices of their most successful private competitors; that, given the choice between raising the dividend or allocating to reserves, societies should do the latter; and that the dividend should be high enough to attract trade, but not so high as to be unsustainable. The report also suggested that societies streamline their management and subcommittee structures.

The Committee of Management of Colchester and East Essex agreed in principle with many of these sentiments, but there was considerable opposition on the part of some individuals to any streamlining of their departmental empires. In accordance with the founding principles of the Co-operative movement, each society was autonomous – excessively so in the view of some people; there was and is no mechanism whereby a centralised policy could be imposed by the Co-operative Union on individual societies. How the recommendations of the report were to be implemented, if at all, was a matter for individual societies. As we shall see, the impact of these decisions would to a large extent dictate the success or failure of many societies, not least Colchester and East Essex, over the next decades.

As the Society reached its centenary year, the future seemed brighter than ever, reflecting the new optimism abroad in Britain as it entered the 1960s. The new shops were light and bright, in some cases boasting escalators and the latest decor. The membership was rising every year, and for every account that was closed, four were opened; by this time, the total exceeded 54,000. Annual sales exceeded £5 million; and the Society's dividend of 1s. was well above the South of England average of 8½d. in the pound. Competition was keen, but so was the spirit of the Society. In accordance with new accounting procedures, quarterly sales figures would no longer be published: 'In the competitive world of retail trading the disclosure of these figures could work very much to our disadvantage,' declared the president in his report to members.

In many ways, he and his colleagues, and the 1,400 employees across the 400 square mile trading area of the Society, had proved themselves equal to the demands of modern business. While remaining true to the traditional principles of co-operation, they more often looked to the future: a future of credit shopping, mobile grocery shops, self-service, financial services and fashion stores 'equal to London standards'. At the same time, they had preserved a management structure that was little changed in 100 years, and many members and staff inherited four generations of family links with the Society. A record 73,000 people crowded into the centenary year Co-operative Exhibition on Holly Trees Meadow in the Castle Park in Colchester during that hot summer, for film shows, fashion displays, cookery demonstrations and performances by the famous CWS (Co-operative Wholesale Society) Prize Band. A celebratory booklet was compiled and printed and went on sale at a modest charge.

Yet, after the band had packed up and gone home, and the exhibition had been dismantled, and the excitement had ended, there

Funeral Services, such as headstone provision, were among the many different ways the Society touched their members' lives.

The Walton Allied shop that opened in 1957 as part of a new Co-op venture to provide shops that sold everything.

Ramsey. The Society's trading area remains mainly rural.

Members inspect part of the complex machinery used for fully automated baking.

remained facts and figures that made sobering reading. Fundamental change was coming to the Co-operative societies, many of which were small and beginning to lose business to the private national retailers, whose obligation to conventional shareholders gave them an even greater competitive impetus. The bigger societies were growing dangerously complacent, with their surpluses, their cautious dividends and their deceptively strong regional identities. Britain was entering a period of unparalleled prosperity, in which the growth of national private retail chains, greater consumer choice and keener competition would not only impinge on the smaller societies, but shake many of the larger ones out of their complacency. This was the beginning of the end of the era of innocence for the Co-operative societies. Those who failed to meet these challenges of change would simply lose their independence and disappear; and this is precisely what would happen to many societies during the 1960s and 1970s. The continued independence and success of Colchester and East Essex Co-op today owes not a little to crucial decisions made by its directors, members and managers of a quarter of a century ago.

4

THE CHALLENGES
OF CHANGE

The Society began the first year of its second century in business with little out of the ordinary to report. In tune with the economic climate of the country as a whole, sales and membership were continuing to grow, and the latest programme of renovations and extensions was under way. The Committee of Management were still congratulating themselves on the success of the centenary celebrations, and on the appointment of one of their number, Councillor Porter, to the office of Mayor of Colchester. However, their serenity would soon be spoiled by a far-reaching event at the heart of the Society: the dismissal of the secretary, Norman Hallmark.

The decision was painful, but necessary. Relations, both personal and professional, had been strained for some time between the secretary and the Committee of Management. He was a full-time paid employee, but had no executive powers; secretaries were all-powerful, but not professional managers in the conventional sense. The secretary wanted modern executive powers, which the departmental managers resisted, and which the Committee were disinclined to grant him. His departure was handled diplomatically, and attracted little outside attention. However, the consequences were significant, for after he left there was no obvious successor. The Committee made a temporary appointment of the assistant secretary, Sidney Orrin, and cast around for a permanent replacement. They found this in J. E. D. (Jack) Owen, general manager of the Parkstone and Bournemouth Society. At the same time, they also

Looking up Trinity Street, Colchester, glimpsing Trinity Church and the Town Hall.

The success of delivering bottled milk is evident in the size of the vehicles now used by milkmen.

decided that, if they were to grant modern executive powers to anyone, this should be to themselves. They began to examine the rules of the Society for ways in which these and other modernising moves could be laid before the members.

The members by this time numbered nearly 60,000, and the Committee were concerned as ever to increase both their number and the turnover, which was currently £100,000 a week: 'It is timely that we should again remind our members of the advantages of the Co-operative Dividend upon purchases,' wrote Dennis Dallender on behalf of the Committee of Management in their latest report to members. 'The many trade-catching "gimmicks" which we see being tried these days fall far short of the financial benefit of the Co-operative Dividend.' These gimmicks were none the less the manifestation of a commercialism and sense of urgency which the Society did not entirely share. In spite of its growing turnover, all financial transactions were still recorded by hand, although there was a machine for signing cheques. Cash takings from shops in central Colchester were brought to head office by hand, through the streets, or by van from the so-called 'town branches'. The country branches often deposited their takings in their local post offices. Aside from the more relaxed attitude to security, there was little perceived need to hurry. As Brian Littlewood, who had recently joined the Society and would become secretary, observed: 'Cash flow was not in the vocabulary of those days.'

The modernisation of Colchester itself was meanwhile gathering pace, and with this came new business opportunities for the Society. A new Town Plan had been published, and, in the aftermath of the exceptionally severe winter of 1963, the Society made representations to Colchester Borough Council concerning sites for new shops on the projected estates. The refitting and extension of shops was also under way in Colchester, Frinton, Tiptree and Clacton-on-Sea. The Society's new garage and showroom opened in Colchester, with the range including low-cost DKW cars imported from what was then East Germany. In order to encourage members to reinvest as much of their half-yearly dividend as possible, a dividend voucher scheme was introduced, whereby these could be redeemed against purchases in the various non-food departments of the Society. Perhaps because of the exceptionally severe winter, the funeral services department was among those showing an increase in profits.

At head office in Victoria Place, a subcommittee of the Management and Education Committees had finished perusing the rule book in pursuit of an organisational structure which would enable them further to modernise the Society. Their recommendations were accepted by the president and the Committee of Management, and adopted after a meeting of members. They included the deletion of the words 'and Industrial' from the full name of the Society; the renaming of the Committee as the 'Board of Directors'; and the streamlining of various subcommittees and reporting procedures. These reforms were achieved despite initial resistance from committee members who feared the loss of their personal territory: 'I was public enemy number one on the Board for some time,' Dennis Dallender recalled. 'But there were far too many subcommittees, and they had to be broken up. It was taking too long to report and implement decisions. I recommended their abolition, and they were up in arms, but we found the solution.' The remedy was to form an executive Board which included, for the first time, both members of the Committee of Management and departmental managers from areas such as grocery, menswear and household goods. This went some way towards eliminating the divisions between the lay management and professional staff, inherent in the old organisation that dated back to 1861. Under this new arrangement, which was unique in the Co-operative movement, the president and Board of Directors would continue to run the Society for some years without a chief executive in the modern sense.

A Co-op hardware delivery van in the early 1960s.

Throughout the second half of the 1960s, Colchester and East Essex Co-op continued to modernise its internal organisation, which had previously lagged behind its forward-looking attitude towards new shops and products. The establishment of the executive Board, and the greater involvement of departmental heads, was followed in 1966 by a reduction both in the number of directors, and of their retirement age. The following year, the Society introduced computerisation for the first time, albeit in a limited way, in the payroll department. Quarterly meetings of members, poorly attended, were reduced to two meetings a year. In 1968, with the retirement of its secretary, the Education Committee was wound up and replaced by a permanent member relations officer and a new Member Relations and Education Department, chaired by the president of the Society. The aim was to preserve the best of the traditional community activities, with a more sophisticated awareness of modern trends and potential for promoting the Co-op brand name.

The butcher's shop of the 1960s and 1970s focused much more on refrigeration and cleanliness.

As Basil Smith, a member of the Board of Directors who had come up through the youth movement and Education Committee route, recalled: 'There is no doubt that at this time the social profile of the "movement" dropped away, and changed with the greater choice that was

Church Street, Harwich, showing St Nicholas Church and the Co-op's Wheatsheaf pub in the 1970s.

available to people. Today, the "movement" ideas of Co-operation have to be, and are, linked to commercial aims. But we have always supported the local community, and we always will. Unlike some private retailers, we do this not just for public relations, we do it for its own sake.'

During these years, the number of shops and the trading area of the Society again grew considerably. In 1967, the secretary of the Harwich, Dovercourt and Parkeston Society, a smaller, but hitherto independently minded Co-op, approached Colchester and East Essex Society with a view to merger. This was not popular with some Harwich, Dovercourt and Parkeston employees, one of whom was Don Barker:

> We had a very strongly capitalised Society and paid 1s. 6d. dividend in the pound, which was more than Colchester and East Essex. We had secured market share and corner sites for new shops. Our quarterly meetings were always packed; we were in close touch with our members. But there were adverse government policies such as Selective Employment Tax, and there was a dock strike. Our sales had plummeted temporarily, and I think our secretary panicked. He need not have sold out, but he did, and so we lost our independence.

Although 135 employees of Harwich, Dovercourt and Parkeston Society remained with Colchester and East Essex Co-op, there were also redundancies. They included Mrs Marjorie Barker. She had been employed to process dividend cheques, which Colchester and East Essex was in the course of replacing with dividend stamps. Also to Don Barker's displeasure, Colchester and East Essex stopped the delivery of bread, centralised the delivery of milk, and closed down the Harwich, Dovercourt and Parkeston-owned pub, the latter a unique phenomenon in the Co-operative movement. As Brian Littlewood, later secretary of Colchester and East Essex Society, observed: 'These days, we would not have closed the pub, we would have made a feature of it.' Barker, meanwhile, was kept on at Harwich by his new employers because of his accounting qualifications.

Barker moved shortly afterwards to Colchester and East Essex Society, where his professional skill did indeed prove useful.

Facing page: Halfpenny Pier at Harwich looking across to Parkeston with the *Splendour of the Seas* in the distance.

Dick Emery promoting the new Co-op dividend stamps and opening Tiptree supermarket during the 1970s.

The Society continued to grow; within a few months it had also absorbed Maldon Society, which maintained small, loss-making stores in remoter parts of the coastal peninsular. Together with Harwich, Dovercourt and Parkeston, this brought the total membership to over 80,000. More new members came as Colchester itself continued to grow. In 1968, with the expansion of the new Greenstead Estate in the town, there at last came planning permission for a supermarket containing a new butchery, cake and confectionery section, chemists shops, and an in-store bakery.

The economy then went into another downturn, and tough times returned yet again for retailers. The new acquisitions and openings were balanced by the closure of loss-making shops and branches at Bures, Tiptree and Walton-on-the-Naze. The Board of Directors of the Society was increasingly using the language of private-sector retailers: 'The Society can only survive as a really successful business,' they wrote to members, 'if uneconomic units and services are curtailed.'

Thus there were further closures, including the grocery and off-licence in Maldon; the grocery and butchery at East Gates, Colchester; the boot and shoe factory in Colchester, in which the Society was a shareholder; the confectionery bakery; the Co-operative laundry, and the small butcher's shops in Long Wyre Street, Rowhedge and Claudius Road: 'These were testing times for the president and the executive Board,' Brian Littlewood recalled. 'Many of the small shops we had acquired through mergers were loss-making, but they served a local need, and we only closed them when new stores were opened up in those areas, either by us or someone else.' Among the casualties were the Society's rural 'Allied' stores, which sold everything from clothes to carpets and ironmongery, albeit in limited quantities: 'They were Aladdin's caves,' Brian Littlewood recalled, 'but stock-taking at somewhere like Tiptree Allied store was a nightmare.'

As part of this process of reassessment, the Society commissioned the Co-operative Wholesale Society Property Development Department to survey and re-evaluate the complicated web of freehold sites it had acquired in the town centre of Colchester over the years, and advise on the best way ahead for its trading services over the coming decade. Plans for new supermarkets and shopping centres across the trading area continued during the late 1960s, and further mergers followed in 1970. Witham Society, like Maldon, was financially sound, with 6,000 members and an annual trade of £500,000, but like many small independent societies it was losing business to larger private retailers and facing rising costs. Both these pressures were relieved by Witham becoming part of Colchester and East Essex. Earl's Colne Society was similarly well managed, but even smaller, with 1,550 members and an annual trade of £250,000. Where once the village had sustained a grocery, butcher's shop, dry goods and menswear services, greater mobility through the car and access to a wider choice of competitors was threatening the Society with extinction.

Frank Williams was managing secretary of Earl's Colne Society at the time. Williams's mother had worked there before him, and he himself had been through Co-operative College and worked briefly for Colchester and East Essex Society. 'Things were becoming diffi-cult,' he recalled:

> The food side was still successful, but other areas were less so. What had been a comprehensive service to the community was not so profitable any more. It became clear that unless something fairly drastic happened, the Society would not continue. That would have been a disaster for the village. So I approached Jack Owen, the secretary of Colchester and East Essex.

The result was the merger, and the food store and pharmacy flour-ish in Earl's Colne to this day. Williams himself became office manager for Colchester and East Essex Co-op, then management accountant, accountant, secretary and financial controller, retiring in 1991. These mergers brought the membership of Colchester and East Essex Society to nearly 100,000 by 1970. This growth by acquisition was timely; for every three new members, two accounts were closed. Indeed, shortly afterwards, and in part due to a periodic clear-out of dormant accounts, more accounts were closed than opened for the first time in the history of the Society. However, the adoption of redeemable dividend stamps, already in use by most of the top fifty societies across the country, proved a success at Colchester and East Essex after an intensive publicity campaign

Noëlle Gordon opened the new supermarket at Dovercourt in the 1970s.

explained their advantages to the membership. The latter had included die-hard opponents, who harkened back to the days when people queued down the street to collect their quarterly dividends in cash, which they would use to buy their chil-dren's shoes or pay their rates.

There was soon another break with tradition. In Colchester, a new development was nearing com-pletion adjacent to the main grocery warehouse at Peartree Road, Stanway, on a site where five roads converged. The new neighbourhood superstore offered a comprehensive range of food and other products on a cash and carry basis, and was the

Facing page: Looking from Sir Isaac's Walk up Eld Lane in Colchester. The new Jewellery store roof is visible at the end of the street.

first of its kind for the Society. Instead of the conventional 'Co-op' name, hitherto uniform for all its outlets, the Society, reflecting the location, chose 'Fiveways'. The superstore opened in 1971, and marked the beginning of the Fiveways brand name within the Colchester and East Essex Co-operative trading area. Today, there are Fiveways supermarkets in Brightlingsea, Burnham-on-Crouch, Clacton-on-Sea, two in Colchester, Dovercourt, Frinton-on-Sea, Manningtree, Tiptree, West Mersea and Witham; however, today they are once more branded Co-op Fiveways.

In the year the first Fiveways opened, despite the disruption caused by the miners' strike, the sales of the Society passed £10 million. Although they were in part generated by rising prices, it was a real increase. There were also wider economic forces at work in favour of the Society: the region suffered rather less from the impact of recession and energy crises than the more industrialised parts of the country. The Society was big enough, and its reserves sufficient, to absorb a proportion of rising costs and to continue with its programme of expansion. As 1972 progressed, the Society purchased and renamed two more supermarkets at Tiptree and Maldon; enlarged existing shops across the trading area; and continued attempts to reach agreement with the local authority over the proposed development of the site in the centre of Colchester.

Thus the Society entered the economic crisis of the mid-1970s in good shape, with 100,000 members and sales of nearly £14 million a year. Its strategy was to combine aggressive cost-cutting and promotional activity with investment in new shops and services. These included double-dividend stamp fortnights, selective sales at the St Nicholas House furniture store, and the hiring of local and national television personalities to open new stores. At the same time, minimarkets and supermarkets were upgraded, new supermarkets were planned and opened and the funeral services business was expanding.

In its community activities, the Society also reflected the rather depressed atmosphere of the country during these turbulent years. The new Member Relations Subcommittee set out its programme, albeit with mixed results. Members' evenings held at Tiptree and Dovercourt were 'anything but a success', as was reported in the autumn of 1974, and the subcommittee was 'disappointed by the extent of the apathy of the general membership of the Society.' As we have seen, this is a recurrent factor in the success or otherwise of the community activities of the Society at times of change and uncertainty in the wider world. The degree of inclination on the part of people to participate in community activities in meaningful numbers, and on a significant level, is often traceable to the state of the economic climate.

In the mid-1970s, inflation was increasing at an alarming rate.

Comedy duo Morecambe and Wise
relaunching the very first Fiveways Store
in Colchester, 1970s.

During the first half of 1975 alone, the price of food rose by over 25
per cent. Household goods rose by over 20 per cent, and clothing
and footwear by over 15 per cent. Higher unemployment and
reduced overtime earnings also meant that members had less money
to spend on non-food items, such as furniture and clothing. For
retailers, the need for sound investment was greater than ever; yet
the best intentions of the Society in this respect sometimes placed it
at odds with the interests of the working man, in whose name the
Society had been founded. When the Society attempted to contain
rising costs by closing two small butcheries and three small groceries, there were vehement protests from members and the shop
workers' trade union. Meanwhile, other societies were being forced
to close down altogether because they could not or would not grasp
business realities: 'Some went down the drain rather than amalgam-
ate,' as Dennis Dallender recalled. Colchester and East Essex was at
this time the highest dividend-stamp-issuing society in the country,
and Dallender and the Board of Directors would shortly decide to
cut the dividend stamp issue from sixty stamps to forty stamps per
pound spent. They also sounded a warning:

> We operate in a world where success is judged by profit,' they wrote to
> members in 1976, 'and where future survival depends upon sufficient of
> that profit being retained to renew the assets of the business and to
> exploit the techniques of trading which in each generation are shown to
> be in demand and to be the most rewarding. At this point of time empha-
> sis is upon large trading units which give rise to lower unit selling costs
> to the benefit of the consumer.

This meant demolishing small, old shops and building new, large
supermarkets in places such as Upper Dovercourt, Wivenhoe and
Holland-on-Sea. A supermarket was leased and a freezer centre added
at Witham. Attempts to reach agreement with the local council over
the redevelopment of the site in the centre of Colchester continued.

Colchester and East Essex was by this time the seventh in rank of net profitability among British Co-operatives, and maintaining this position was no easy matter; the Society had been ranked as high as third only the previous year. The need was for greater and greater size, simply in order to maintain existing reserves in the face of rising inflation. With a departmental structure increasingly inadequate to handle the size and complexity of the business, the pace of growth began to worry the president and Board of Directors: 'I could see a point coming when we wouldn't be able to cope any longer,' Dennis Dallender recalled, 'so the secretary, Mr Owen, and I went to Sweden, where they had a very progressive approach to Co-operative societies, to study how they handled this kind of problem there.'

Terry Wogan signs autographs for members at the Maldon High Street supermarket opening in 1972.

Dallender and Owen learned much during their visit, and, with the vice-president Basil Smith and other members of the Board, they produced a report concerning the future management structure of Colchester and East Essex Society. Their findings were summarised in a single recommendation: they should appoint the Society's first full-time professional chief executive:

> Again, there was a lot of opposition [recalled Dallender], but I felt it was necessary if the Society was to survive. It took a long time to persuade some people; they were afraid of losing power. But different managers were pulling in different directions, and I thought we should have someone at the top to hold the whole thing together. One of our best managers threatened to leave if a chief executive came in. He eventually stayed until retirement. But these things caused a lot of concern and upset at the time. It was one of the hardest battles I had to fight, but I was convinced it was right for the Society.

Dr David Bellamy attending the 1979 Co-op Day.

This was a key decision in the modern story of the Society, marking a break with 117 years of tradition and the beginning of the present era. The Board's choice as chief executive was Derek Round. Round had worked with the Netherfield, Nottingham, King's Lynn, Ipswich and Plymouth Co-operative Societies, and had experience in private retailing both in Britain and overseas. In 1978, after a period as Dry Goods Trades Officer with Colchester and East Essex, he was appointed to the job:

> The Society was going through quite a traumatic time [Round recalled]. It was basically a sound business

enterprise, but trading profits had gone down by 50 per cent. The departmental managers had tremendous knowledge, but they had been used to controlling their own destinies, and they had to be welded together. The shops varied tremendously in standards of environment, quality of merchandise and staff motivation. It was a situation which many societies were probably facing at the time.

I had a tacit agreement with the president and Board that I had total power. But you can't appeal for loyalty; you have to earn it. So my message was that we had to create a team, to generate interdependence as opposed to independence. In other words, to co-operate.

A typical weather-boarded cottage at West Mersea.

This appeal for greater team spirit was given added urgency by the continuing effects of the crisis in the country as a whole. The first months of 1979 saw the worst winter for many years, strikes by transport and public sector workers, spiralling interest rates, panic buying of foods and a general slump in consumer confidence. The troubled economic climate meant

that the Society's decision to borrow money against its assets – a step deemed necessary at the time if the Co-op was to go forward – was achieved at a considerable cost: 'The first eighteen months were tough,' Round recalled. 'We had to take calculated risks about our growth and the future. You also have to do a few things that have visible impact very quickly. So we created greater openness; people were encouraged to come forward with problems before they got out of hand.'

Shortly after the appointment of a chief executive, work began, after a long delay, on the development of a new department store in Long Wyre Street in the centre of Colchester. In addition to Roman remains already known to be present on the site, the Colchester Archaeological Trust discovered a previously unknown Roman Street, an echo of life as it had been in the oldest recorded town. The Long Wyre Street archaeologists made these and other discoveries with the help of a donation from Colchester and East Essex Society.

The development of Long Wyre Street was long-awaited good

Even on the sparsely populated island of Mersea the Co-op has the primary food outlet.

The Colchester store, Culver Street, in the 1970s.

news, amidst the freezing weather and chill winds of the political and economic climate; the latter, at least, was on the brink of change. A new era was beginning under the Conservative government of Margaret Thatcher, herself the daughter of a shopkeeper, but whose version of self-help was much at variance with that of Co-operative societies.

Shares & Dividends

Members may buy and hold shares in the Society, both as an investment offering a modest but secure return, and as a sign of their support for its general business ethos. In keeping with the democratic structure of the Society, and unlike PLCs, the size of an individual shareholding makes no difference to the weight of an individual member's vote.

The dividend paid annually to members is entirely independent of any shareholding they may also hold. It is calculated according to the amount of their purchases and the profitability of the Society in the year in question.

5

CO-OPERATION
AND COMPETITION

Colchester and East Essex Co-op entered the 1980s amidst tough trading conditions, but with the cautious optimism that characterised the country at large. The membership had risen to nearly 114,000, and once more a greater number of people were joining rather than leaving the Society. The new department store in the town centre, referred to in the previous chapter, was nearing completion. Opened by the president, Dennis Dallender, in the autumn of 1980, it was the largest development ever undertaken by the Society. In more depressed parts of the country, other societies and private retailers were closing branches, reducing staff and work hours, cutting or ceasing dividends and suspending community involvement. By contrast, the Society was opening and reopening new and modernised shops and supermarkets, and selling a wider range of foods and goods which was presented with a brighter image and a higher public profile.

Within the Society, the new management structure meant that all departments, operations, employees, managers, finances, reporting relationships, services and values were subject to re-evaluation; great efforts were made to carry this out in the Co-operative spirit. Staff were given better training, and encouraged to feel that they belonged to an organisation that was going places. As Derek Round recalled: 'We wanted people to know what was happening, this year, next year, the year after. Then, when better results come through, people realise it is working. You instil the joys of capitalism in people.'

Across the trading area, these joys included the strengthening of the 'Co-op' name by co-ordinating in-store promotional materials, and attempting to take the flagship department stores upmarket. The 'Fiveways' principle was extended beyond the single superstore of that name, to a brand identity for similar stores in other

neighbourhoods, large enough to support the trade, but not of sufficient size to attract competition from the national retail chains. Other societies, also perceiving the 'Co-op' name as weak in brand terms, also introduced specialist stores under new names at this time. Today, however, the name 'Co-op Fiveways' shows that the 'Co-op' brand has been reclaimed by Colchester and East Essex Society as a positive asset.

The opening of the Co-op Department Store in the town centre of Colchester was one of the last acts undertaken as president by Dennis Dallender, who retired in 1981 after twenty-five years in the role, and over fifty years with the Co-operative movement. Jack Owen, the long-serving secretary, also retired at this time, and was succeeded by Frank Williams. The new president, Basil Smith, unlike Dallender was independently employed outside the Society, in his case as a farmer. Like Dallender, however, he was steeped in the Co-operative movement, and looked ahead with a moderniser's mind: 'This was a period of tremendous growth,' Smith recalled. 'The job took up a lot of time, and I enjoyed every minute of it.'

Growth was accompanied by the modernisation of stores and goods, coupled with high-profile marketing. The Society's sales in 1982 for the first time exceeded £50 million, or £1 million a week, albeit fuelled by continuing inflation; this was twice the national average increase in turnover of Co-operative societies. In pursuit of lower costs and bulk purchasing, Colchester and East Essex Society combined with the Chelmsford and Ipswich Societies, with both of whom it would discuss merging over the years, to establish a federal food warehouse and distribution centre. In time, the centre would supply over 7,000 food lines to all the food shops of the three societies.

By this time, Colchester was being seen by the national retail chains as a desirable place to compete for business. Local retailers were also becoming rivals for the range of goods supplied by the Co-op. Heightened competition became a greater factor in the planning decisions of the Society. Customer loyalty could never be taken for granted, least of all in the environment of economic uncertainty prevailing during the early 1980s. In an effort to maintain this loyalty, more money was returned to members in the form of dividend stamps, and greater attempts were made to promote the Society through its activities in the community. New members were given a detailed information pack about the Co-op and its commercial and community activities. The amount and quality of advertising increased to such a degree, that, in 1983, Colchester and East Essex Co-op was awarded the CWS Advertising Trophy.

At the same time, there was the acknowledgement that certain traditional means of communication were no longer appropriate. Where, for example, there had been frequent meetings of members

Facing page: Tollesbury Marina.

The CWS Advertising Trophy, won by the Society in 1983.

Basil Smith (then president) assists Diana Dors in signing autographs on Co-op Day in 1981.

An early Electronix store, a new venture by the Society to bring themselves up-to-date with the explosion in electrical appliances.

across the trading area, dwindling attendance resulted in the number and frequency being reduced to a more appropriate level.

If national and local retailers were competing to match the range of goods supplied by the Society, the Society could respond by extending its own range of goods and services. Through 1983 and 1984, the Co-op accordingly opened new jewellery and 'Home-maker' stores in Clacton-on-Sea, and its first camera and computer shop in Long Wyre Street, Colchester. More shops and services were upgraded and expanded, again with the aim of pre-empting competition: 'We were buying shops and sites partly in order to put off other buyers,' Derek Round recalled. This strategy sometimes antagonised smaller local retailers, who saw Colchester and East Essex Society in the same way as they perceived the national retail chains as a threat to their livelihoods. The new Fiveways stores projected for Burnham-on-Crouch and Brightlingsea, for example, provoked this kind of reaction. However, as secretary Frank Williams recalled: 'Opening a bigger food store there was beneficial in the end, both to local people and local shopkeepers. Where they had once had to go outside Burnham, they could now do their food shopping locally. This meant they shopped locally for other things, too.'

In such a competitive atmosphere, there was less likelihood than ever that the customer would limit his or her shopping to a single source of supply. Membership of the Co-op did not inhibit members from shopping elsewhere, either in parallel with the Co-op, or as a direct alternative. Co-op sales rose, but membership slowly but steadily began to fall back to just below 100,000 (although it has since climbed back to over 150,000). At that time, however, the national retail chains, with the help of their lavishly funded television advertising campaigns, were quick to adopt 'loyalty' devices of the kind pioneered by the Co-operative societies, and trumpet these as if they were their own. Colchester and East Essex Co-op was by this time outperforming much of the rest of the Co-operative movement, but the movement as a whole was losing market share. These forces would have a profound and unsettling influence on Colchester and East Essex Society, and all Co-ops, over the remainder of the decade.

The independence of Colchester and East Essex Co-op today does not mean that in the past it has not contemplated merger with neighbours. In 1985, these included the Greater Peterborough and Waveney Societies, with whom the Society entered into talks aimed at forming a joint Anglia Co-operative Society. The talks led to the formation of a holding society designed to enable joint trading, development and marketing; the proposed three-way merger, however, did not ma-terialise. The following year, in 1986, the directors of Ipswich Society approached Colchester and East Essex, again with a view to merger; the two societies were already linked through the federal food warehouse. These talks were equally extensive, and a tentative date was set for the end of the decade; again, however, no merger ensued.

A pancake race in Colchester, organised by the Society in 1985.

During this period, the recession lifted and consumer confidence returned, reducing the pressure to merge and bringing with it the momentum to take the Society forward again. At the same time, where once it had been relatively insulated from the fortunes of the rest of the country, Colchester and East Essex was becoming one of the fastest expanding regions in Britain. Commercial and residential developments were under way which other retailers were keen and able to exploit. The Society would face even greater competition and would no longer enjoy unchallenged opportunities of the kind which had contributed to its growth during the early years.

The 125th anniversary was celebrated in 1986 with a wide variety of activities, a double bonus on dividend stamps and share accounts, and a visit by members to the Toad Lane Museum in Rochdale, the birthplace of the Co-operative movement. The Rochdale Society remained in existence only as part of a larger regional group oper-ated by Co-operative Retail Services (CRS). Rochdale itself was a poignant reminder of a glorious history gradually superseded by the decline of the industrial north, a process in which strength of com-munity had not been enough to triumph over economic collapse. Colchester and East Essex Co-op, meanwhile, was looking ahead once more, in this case demonstrating its faith in the future with a new Fiveways store at Dovercourt, the first 'Electronix' centre at Fiveways in Colchester, new developments at Witham and Kelvedon and the launch of an expanded travel service.

By 1988, although the annual turnover of the Society had nearly

A Co-op store fashion brochure from the 1980s.

Co-op Day in 1986 coincided with the Society's 125th anniversary celebrations, including this colourful 'birthday cake' float.

doubled to £100 million in five years, costs were escalating, margins falling and the generous dividend was becoming untenable. However, the ability to go on opening new superstores and offer a wider range of quality products, was seen as crucial to sustaining this growth. As a result, new Fiveways superstores were under development at Witham, Frinton, and Mersea; new Electronix centres would shortly open in Colchester, Dovercourt and Clacton-on-Sea; and the travel services and motor trade continued to grow. The Society was also introducing many other customer-friendly innovations worthy of a modern brand name. These included in-store pharmacies, credit cards and in-store banking (subsequently supplemented by the Co-operative Bank's adoption of Automated Teller Machines).

For Colchester and East Essex Society, this period in its story was characterised by the willingness of Derek Round and his colleagues boldly to grasp the opportunities presented by a rising economy. The economic boom of the late 1980s was unprecedented in modern times, and the Co-op was determined to enjoy the benefits along with everyone else. Yet, these external forces were to be at the root of the problems that followed. History bears witness that all boom times are inevitably followed by an equally dramatic downturn, or 'bust'. Only when the latter occurs, as it must do, do the fundamental strengths of an organisation come to the fore. For the Co-op, these strengths were in its underlying soundness, its market presence, coupled with value for money, and in the experience and loyalty of nearly 2,000 members of staff across a trading area of 600 square miles.

Another attribute would be called upon in the difficult times that lay ahead; this was the ability of the Society to identify its faults. The 1990s would see a number of large regional societies fail to do so and reluctantly exchange their independence for life under the umbrella of the Co-operative Wholesale Society (CWS). For Colchester and East Essex Co-op, their ability to analyse and correct their weaknesses, was perhaps their most important strength.

However, at the time, it seemed that the Society could do no wrong. Chris Blanchett would shortly take up the new appointment of retail controller, effectively deputy chief executive, and ultimately successor to Derek Round. Blanchett lived locally, but his career included the national retail PLCs: 'In the 1980s retailers everywhere were opening shops at an unsustainable rate and in many cases regardless of cost. However, the seemingly limitless sales fuelling this boom was, in reality, being driven by a double figure inflation.' Colchester Co-op was no exception and as the Society entered the 1990s, few were prepared for the bumpy ride that lay ahead.

6

RECESSION AND RECOVERY

Given the suddenness and severity of the downturn of the early 1990s, the fact that the Society had survived many similar crises was a reassurance. There had been early opposition to its existence, two World Wars, the inter-war Depression, the great shake-out of Co-operative societies during the 1960s and 1970s and other difficult times. It had made a successful transition from a lay Committee of Management and secretary, to a modern-minded Board of Directors and management structure headed by a professional chief executive. In the early and middle 1980s, it had shown it could behave like a conventional retailer where necessary, and pursued growth with vigour and panache across East Essex. History, however, does not pay the bills, and the bills were mounting.

In the late 1980s, the Co-op, like other retailers, had pursued growth in conditions of increasing inflation. Unlike private retailers, the Society, as we have seen, was not able to raise funds through

Below left: The Tour de Tendring bicycle ride's joint sponsorship by the Society and Kimberley Clark raised £45,000 for the RNLI.
Below: A girl proudly shows off her certificate to prove she cycled 20 miles.

Another beneficiary of the Society's strong community relations was Colchester Swimming Club which received £600 in 1993.

The Society's staff fundraising activities raised £12,000 for the local hospital's Raise A Laser appeal.

outside shareholders and the stock markets. The new stores were being funded by loans from the Co-operative Bank and by 1990 borrowings were rising dramatically. The Report and Accounts for 1991 revealed a disturbing trend. Although sales were at an all-time high, of the £4.7 million trading profit generated that year only £104,000 remained after interest on loans and members dividends had been paid. Gearing was approaching 120 per cent and interest rates were rising. In the shops, sales of essential, low-margin goods such as foodstuffs remained steady; in traditionally more profitable departments, such as furniture and electronic equipment, however, sales fell steeply and reflected the general cutback in consumer spending. The economic downturn meant that development had already slowed considerably, although construction was under way of Fiveways supermarkets at Brightlingsea and Manningtree. As the recession continued and deepened, unemployment rose, house prices plummeted and stories of repossessions and negative equity filled the newspaper headlines. By 1991, the boom envisaged for the 1990s was becoming a bad dream for retailers.

Chris Blanchett had been taking the opportunity of his first months with the Co-op to learn about the trading activities of the Society: 'The organisation was so diverse,' he recalled. 'What sort of business has travel centres and dairies and funeral services? I had been a little sceptical at first, but there was a tremendous tangibility, and something different, about this major regional Co-op.' He was beginning to grasp the complexities of this organisation, but was looking forward to a period of further acclimatisation, when Derek Round announced he wished to take early retirement. Within only a few months of his arrival, and two years earlier than he had anticipated, Blanchett became chief executive-designate at a crucial point in the fortunes of the Society.

The gloomy outlook reflected in the 1990 accounts was now a reality. Trading profits for 1991 were £4.7 million, but of the total, £2.5 million would be consumed by interest and £1.5 million paid out in dividends: 'You didn't have to be a brilliant mathematician,' Blanchett recalled, 'to see that there wasn't much left.' Blanchett was also aware, however, that he was a newcomer. The Board of Directors had accepted his predecessor's early retirement with reluctance, and they were still coming to terms with the full implications of the sudden downturn in business. But it was clear that firm action was required:

The pace of change is critical in an organisation like this

[Blanchett recalled] The most important feature of my first two years was the building of trust and relationships. Had I come in and attempted to achieve all the things I achieved over four or five years, in a single year, it would have ended in tears.

I had to demonstrate to the Board, step by step, that if big and hard decisions are managed properly, things will end up for the better. Not only that, but it is the role of the modern chief executive to handle exactly these problems.

So, on the one hand I had to be diplomatic, but on the other hand there was a critical situation.

Electronic scanning using the latest technology.

Blanchett was helped by the fundamental soundness of the Society. He also enjoyed the support of the new secretary, Brian Littlewood, and the president, Basil Smith, who was succeeded in 1992 by Donald Munson. With trading conditions by this time at their worst for several decades, the need to combine diplomacy with decisiveness was paramount. During 1992, the Personnel and Training Department carried out an evaluation that resulted in the reclassification of 1,200 members of staff. This opened up new opportunities for training and career development. Staff were also paid a bonus in acknowledgement of their efforts during these difficult times. The need to concentrate on profit rather than sales and to cut back capital spending and expenses, could be turned to the advantage of the Society. Smaller shops were refurbished at relatively low cost, and the more labour-intensive aspects of customer service were reviewed. Information technology was introduced at the point of sale: 'We made this cost-cutting period work for us,' Blanchett recalled, 'in that it gave us a breathing space. We concentrated on improving day-to-day standards and becoming better retailers.'

In the community, the Co-op and its Member Relations Department were finding a new demand for their services: 'Co-operation in general took a back seat in the roaring eighties,' Brian Littlewood observed. The new management, however, recognised the benefits of focused community activity and charity work as being consistent with successful trading.

Fiercely competitive trading conditions led to national supermarket chains flouting the law on Sunday trading. Colchester and East Essex Co-op initially resisted the temptation, only succumbing with reluctance just before Christmas, when it opened selected stores, as the Directors put it, 'to protect the Society's market share'. The increase in sales to £162 million for the year was encouraging, especially as it had been achieved without resorting to Sunday trading for most of this time, and considering that some fresh food prices had fallen by as much as 20 per cent.

With the heat having been taken out of the economy, inflation

The Essex Fire and Rescue Service run a trauma Teddy scheme with the Society that provides a teddy for children in the event of a fire or accident to help minimise their trauma.

Dividend book and stamps.

was now at its lowest rate for twenty-five years. The Society was growing again in real terms, although its fixed costs continued to outstrip inflation. With major developments placed on hold, discount schemes in operation and staff and small shops undergoing training and refurbishment, the Co-op still needed 'to get back to basics,' as Chris Blanchett put it, 'and that's no bad thing for a retailer.'

There was one trading activity which seemingly could not be brought into profit, however great the effort made by all concerned. The retail motor division was most sensitive to recession, and it also sat the least comfortably with the other businesses. Its sale would remove a loss-making business from the revenue account, and generate funds to reduce the indebtedness of the Society at a stroke. The wisdom of this was plain, but there were obstacles. The sense of responsibility ran deep on the part of the Co-op towards staff and their families, even in loss-making areas of the business. The sale might result in redundancies, not to mention bad publicity. The Co-op started to look for a buyer through whom it could avoid both these consequences.

Continuing introduction of new information technology, meanwhile, substantially reduced operating costs, even in the smallest shops. In a Co-op supermarket, the benefit was enormous. There might be as many as 700 price changes in a single week; with manual price labelling, they were difficult to co-ordinate and there was no way of measuring the volume of business from moment to moment. Electronic price scanning was an inexpensive and labour-saving solution, which improved security and gave the Society greater control over its business. The Fiveways stores were electronically linked to a common price file, managed by a central computer at the headquarters of the Food Division. This was followed by a similar linkage of every food shop, great and small, across the region. These innovations reduced costs and labour-intensiveness, improving efficiency and most importantly, customer service. By 1994, the Co-op would have extended computerised inventory controls into funeral services, travel centres and pharmacies. Within two years, from being an organisation without a single word processor at head office, the Society became the leading Co-operative in the country to apply information technology across its shops and services to such a degree.

During this time, inflation remained low and price competition keen, enabling the Society to continue to grow in real terms. In 1993, a year of further deep recession, sales reached nearly £170 million, the equivalent to customer spending of nearly £1,000 for every household in the trading area.

Even the retail motor division was showing signs of improvement. However, the Co-op took advantage of this to agree the sale of the motor trade, almost without redundancies and for a substantial sum, to the kind of buyer it had been seeking, namely the Ipswich and Norwich Co-operative Society. The sale was concluded in 1994, and the proceeds reduced the indebtedness of the Co-op by 20 per cent, reducing the turnover, but increasing the profitability of the Society. As Chris Blanchett recalled, 'not only did the sky not fall in' as a result of this major disposal, it actually created a greater trust and understanding with the Board of Directors. Closer links also began to develop with the Society's partners, the Co-operative Wholesale Society and the Co-operative Bank; and Blanchett, like his predecessor, would be appointed to the Board of Directors of both organisations. This kind of teamwork brought a greater shared awareness of the Co-op's strengths and strategies, which in its turn encouraged further ideas and made future decision-making easier. Following the success of the computerised linkage of shops and supermarkets, management took a fresh look – again with the help of information technology – at a fundamental feature of the Co-op, and of the Co-operative system: the dividend.

The Society decided to return to one of the founding principles of Co-operation, by reinstating the dividend as a privilege available only to registered members, a move which would result in an influx of 15,000 new members. However, there was more to be done if the

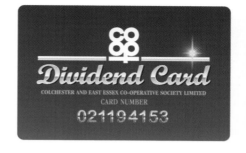

In 1994 the Society launched a dividend swipe card instead of issuing stamps. This was part of a larger scheme to modernise the technology of the Society as a whole.

Making deliveries in Colchester and the surrounding area.

The Fiveways Tiptree 10-Mile Road Race takes place annually with races for both adults and children.

The start of the Children's race.

dividend was truly to reflect the balance between growth and profitability. This was to tread on hallowed ground: 'Dividend is what the Co-op is all about,' Chris Blanchett recalled. 'Tamper with it, and you are living dangerously. So how on earth do you persuade the Board, let alone the membership, that it should be reduced?' Yet there were powerful arguments that such a move would reinforce the first responsibility of the Society: to provide the best possible shops and services at the best possible value for its members.

The answer to the question of how to reform the dividend came about fortuitously, in the way in which it was delivered. This had long taken the form of dividend stamps, dispensed during the course of the year in large quantities to shoppers whether or not they were Co-op members, and regardless of the actual profitability of the Society. This outdated and inefficient practice provided the opportunity to modernise the dividend as a whole. From 1994, instead of stamps, computerised swipe cards would operate in conjunction with the electronic price-scanning being installed at the Co-op's points of sale. No more stamps would be issued once the existing supply had been exhausted, and all members would have to re-register in order to qualify for the card. This would have the additional benefit of ascertaining more precisely the size of the active membership. Furthermore, the level of dividend would henceforth be declared only after the year-end profits were known. The Society was thus freed from being hostage to a pre-set dividend. Since that time, the dividend has been declared only after the calculation has been made of the amount of profit needed to reinvest in the business. The size of the dividend compares favourably with that of conventional public limited companies.

The Co-op gained a large amount of favourable press coverage with the introduction of the dividend card, the ultra-modern appearance of which had a positive effect on the shopper. Colchester and East Essex Co-op was the first Society to introduce such a card, and in calculating the dividend in this flexible way it is still unique in the Co-operative movement. It has subsequently been copied by at least one national retail chain.

In the following year, 1995, the continuing drive for better cost control and higher margins led the Society to join the Co-operative Society Retail Trading Group. This organisation accounted for approximately 65 per cent of all Co-op food buying, amounting to £3 billion a year. The move placed Colchester and East Essex Co-op in a better position to compete with the national retailers moving into its trading area, and increased the range of Co-op 'own brand' products on sale in its shops. As a result, the Co-op's net profits before distribution rose to £2.8 million, in spite of lower sales of £153 million. A dividend of £350,000, or 20 per cent of post-tax profits, was shared between 71,000 registered members. By 1996, this number would have risen to nearly 100,000, and the dividend would shortly also be extended to all Fiveways supermarkets and petrol forecourts.

The recession and recovery of the first half of the 1990s were defining experiences for the Society. The challenges posed, and the solutions produced, speak volumes, not just about the commitment and resourcefulness of the Directors and Officers, but about the effort and adaptability of all the employees, many of whom had spent the greater part of their working lives with the Co-op.

For trading conditions remained difficult, competition continued to grow, and prices to fall; special promotions were frequently employed across many of the shops, placing an additional workload on employees. In addition, selective refurbishment had taken place, new training standards and technology systems had been applied and yet all the while a tight rein was kept on expenditure. The recovery from recession was as much due to the introduction of these measures and the contribution of employees in implementing continued cost-savings, as it was to any improvement in the economy as a whole.

Likewise, the good working relationship between the president and chief executive was an important factor during these times of change. In 1994, Donald Munson retired from the role and was succeeded by Brian Barton. Barton, like his predecessors, had a deep appreciation both of the Co-operative heritage and of the need to look ahead. Since the appointment of the first independent chief executive nearly twenty years earlier, there had been a clear allocation of responsibilities in the boardroom in Victoria Place. The executive officers are responsible for the commercial operations of the Society, while the Board of Directors represent the interests of members and put into practice its community ideals. This requires not only good intentions, but ever greater expertise. Members of the Co-op Board of Directors now attend business training courses at the Society's own premises and at the Co-operative College, and the majority are members of the Institute of Co-operative Directors (ICD).

As the first half of the 1990s came to an end, and the first fruits of recovery became visible, the role of the Co-op once more came under scrutiny. To what extent can a modern trading organisation play a meaningful part in the social and cultural life of the community? What is the relationship between a successful independent Co-operative Society, and the centralised Co-operative 'movement'? The second half of the decade would suggest some answers.

The sponsorship of playgroups is a major concern of the Member Relations Committee.

The Member Relations Committee. Left to right: Gillian Bober, Chairman; James Day (Secretary) Management Representative, and Jackie Bowis (Member Relations Officer) Secretary to Committee.

7

Facing page: Deliveries to Co-op Fiveways supermarket, Abbots Road, Colchester.

A TRADITION OF TRADE

Now in a secure position to go forward again, the Co-op opened new services and shops. In 1996, these included a travel desk at the Fiveways supermarket in Clacton-on-Sea and an elegant new jewellery store in Witham. At Dovercourt, the Society's Department Store was completely refurbished, and work was under way on a 5,000 sq. ft extension to the Fiveways supermarket, to be renamed 'Co-op Fiveways Dovercourt'. Food stores were extensively renovated at Colchester Prettygate and Silver End, both of these representing major investments in local communities.

With the decision to join the Co-operative Retail Trading Group, the Co-op was buying foodstuffs on better terms and thus maintaining competitive prices in the shops. The continued decline in demand for doorstep delivery of milk prompted the Co-op to exchange milk rounds and allied services with its competitors; this created a more efficient business that gave better service to the doorstep customer. At the same time, the Co-op rebalanced its dairy operations by purchasing other existing retail and semi-retail dairy businesses, which brought new customers, employees, depots and vehicle fleets to the Society. The biggest single move forward was

The Homemaker store, Stanway, Colchester.

Furniture delivery to a customer's home.

planned for the town from which the Co-op takes its name. For some time, the management had been carrying out a detailed review of the Society's property portfolio. A considerable amount of valuable property was deemed to be lying dormant and suitable for sale. With the Co-op's borrowings greatly reduced, and lower interest rates in operation, the proceeds could be reinvested. Properly 're-cycled', this surplus property could realise sufficient funds to enable work to begin on a £10 million retail development programme, much of this on the Co-op's doorstep.

The programme included the remodelling and doubling in size of the Homemaker/Electronix store in Peartree Road, Colchester, in response to the continuing trend towards furniture and electronic goods shopping on edge of town locations. A new Co-op Fiveways supermarket would also be built in Abbot's Road, Colchester, a development planned before the recession. Most ambitiously, the Co-op planned the radical rearrangement of its department store in the town centre, and a major new development for retail tenants on the land next to Eld Lane.

The stimulus for this new development was not merely the availability of funds. Shopping habits had changed since the existing stores had been opened. The Co-op needed to reorganise its shopping space to meet contemporary needs. The 90,000 sq. ft department store was too large and insufficiently smart for contemporary requirements. The plan was to demolish one half of the building and reconfigure the other half with air conditioning, automatic doors and elevators, and a café. The surplus space was to be used for the retail development. The proliferation of out-of-town stores also meant that St Nicholas House was no longer appropriate for its original purpose as a furniture store, and would be sold. A ramshackle property currently let on a peppercorn rent on the corner of Victoria Place and Eld Lane would also be demolished, and a new showpiece jewellery store built on the site. In all these new Co-op shops, there would be greater uniformity of standards of presentation and more appropriate allocation of space. In addition, ownership of the retail development would yield valuable rental income for the Co-op and its members through future recessions and recoveries, contributing both to its long-term financial security and its yearly dividend.

This was the largest development undertaken in Colchester by the Co-op since the late 1950s, and with its completion the Co-op had once again made a major impact on the townscape. The scale and diversity of the scheme meant that financial appraisals and planning consents would take the best part of a year to complete. Over the same period, through 1997, major openings by competitors took place across the trading area which had a negative effect on the Society's performance at a time when its operations were already being disrupted by its own development programme.

In spite of these difficult circumstances the Co-op's shops and services not only increased sales by £2 million but most importantly retained profits for reinvestment. Even after returning nearly 20 per cent of the profit to Members, net profit before tax was up to £3.5 million.

This provided the basis for funding yet more developments. A major new supermarket in Colchester was started and a programme of extending and upgrading the others commenced. In all, the Society would invest £10 million in developments during 1998.

In the centre of the town, the partial demolition and reorganisation of the department store, the construction of the

Below left: Mersea Island Primary School collected a record number of vouchers entitling them to free musical instruments as part of the Co-op National Music for Schools campaign, and acquired a musical instrument for every pupil in the school.
Below right: West Mersea Lifeboat crew were given a TV for training purposes as a result of the Society's sponsorship.

During the redevelopment of the department store in Long Wyre Street, Colchester, (*above right*), archaeologists discovered Roman pots and implements (*above left*) and the remains of a Roman mosaic road (*below*), all of which were excavated and recorded before the building work resumed.

jewellery store and the investment development in Long Wyre Street were under way. An anchor tenant had been secured for the main retail unit, and tenants were expected to begin trading by the summer of 1999. By this time, the Co-op would also have established its own property division, and acquired more property in the centre of the town.

The general reinvigoration and expansion of the Co-op and its image was also reflected in its sponsorship of community events across the region. The Member Relations Department sought to set up new youth activities in line with the Society's historical commitment to a wider social purpose. This involvement in the community was complemented by the Public Relations Department.

If the image of the Co-op at the community level is being presented in a more conscious and focused way, there are still occasions on which it comes into conflict with perceptions that date back to a previous era. The most common misconception is that Colchester and East Essex Co-op is a regional 'branch' of a national retail giant known as 'The Co-op', when in fact the Society is totally independent. Other assumptions about the Co-op belie its ability to change with the times. The proposed closure of the loss-making store in Wimpole Road, Colchester, for example, aroused intense passions which were summed up by the remark of an elderly lady interviewed for the local paper: 'I don't shop there myself,' she volunteered, 'but I think they should keep it open.' During the anti-veal calf shipment demonstrations at the port of Brightlingsea, the management and staff of the Co-op store there scrupulously maintained their displays of fresh free range and naturally reared meat products, as befitting its position as a responsible retailer. However, it is interesting to note that the sale of cigarettes, whisky and pork pies

The new jewellery store, Eld Lane, Colchester, which was completed in December 1997.

benefited most from this temporary swelling of the population. During the same protests at Brightlingsea, the Co-op was accused on different occasions of bias towards both the police and the protestors – a curious situation for a Co-op which had resisted even breaking the law over Sunday trading. It is difficult to imagine these reactions being provoked by a conventional private retailer.

The Co-op development in the town centre of Colchester, and the new openings across East Essex, are significant steps forward, but they are only the latest investments for the future of the Society and its members. The ability of the Co-op to reinvent itself for new generations is part of a tradition of trade in which mutual ownership and enterprise are partners in a unique kind of prosperity. The achievements of this partnership over the 1990s suggest the likely role it can play in the customer-based community during the first years of the new millennium.

8

YOUR SOCIETY:
LOOKING AHEAD

One hundred and thirty-eight years ago, a pioneering group of people came together to solve a problem. In doing so, they created an enterprise which has proved capable of adapting to meet the needs of successive and very different generations. Today, it is a major independent organisation owned by its 150,000 members, with 2,000 employees and annual sales of £160 million. Beginning as a single shop, open three evenings a week to sell flour and bread, it is now a regional trading organisation with over eighty trading locations across 600 square miles of Colchester and East Essex. Goods and services range from modern supermarkets and village food shops to department stores, travel centres, restaurants, pharmacies, electricals, furniture and furnishings, jew-

Below left: Milk delivery.
Below right: Delivering pharmaceutical supplies to a local nursing home.

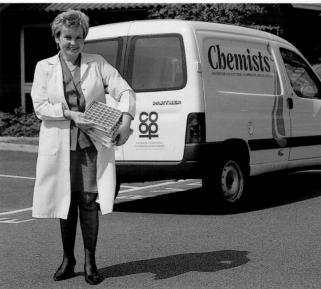

ellery, funeral services and milk. This diversity is unmatched by any other retailer in the area, and yet the Co-op believes it can match all of them for quality.

At the same time, the Co-op is committed to applying its founding principles in new and relevant ways. Chris Blanchett, the chief executive, speaks for the Society: 'We do not wish to run a successful business which is not a co-operative; nor a co-operative which is not a successful business.'

The Co-op flourishes independently today, because its present form encompasses the experience of so many challenges and opportunities met by committed and enterprising people over the years. The decisions of the founders and their successors, the events and choices in the lives of their members over the years, were as influential at the time as the actions of the directors, managers and employees of the Co-op are today. Moreover, in today's climate of consumer choice and an emphasis on ethical values, the Co-op can offer a unique advantage to its customers. The Co-op is committed to responsible retailing as part of its long-held founding principles, and not simply as a public relations exercise. Fair trading, clear and honest presentation and ethical sourcing of products are and will always be as important as high standards of service, convenience and value for money. This is possible because the Co-op is run on the most modern business lines, and also because it is free from obligation to City investors and profit-takers. The Co-op makes its own decisions first and foremost in the interests of its members and customers. It trades in close co-operation with the Co-operative Wholesale Society and the Co-operative Bank. But unlike big national chains, it remains locally owned and independent.

Above left: Funeral Services are provided by the Society.
Above right: Instore staff training.

Over the years, most people's lives in Colchester and East Essex have been touched by the Co-op, and this story aims to show why. In the words of Graham Bober, a director for eighteen years and elected president in 1999:

I hope you have enjoyed reading this book. It's about a local success story, involving numerous individuals committed to upholding the finest values of co-operative collective ownership, and aspiring to trade in a hostile environment, yet attempting to apply the highest ethical values.

We are a people's business, and will, I hope, remain in the vanguard of co-operative enterprise. The current board is deeply indebted to all those past and present employees, member shareholders and shoppers who have, and continue to, loyally support this, their locally owned business.

In a world economy, dominated and manipulated by a powerful minority, the potential power of the consumer can be marshalled for the greater good. Democratic control and accountability through the intelligent use of co-operative enterprise, mutuality and co-ownership can be tailored to meet and beat the challenge, providing an exciting and worthwhile framework for those about to step out from the past into the twenty-first century.

The new Society president, seated centre, and his four predecessors.
Dennis Dallender (seated right) October 1955–April 1981
Basil Smith (seated left) April 1981–April 1993
Don Munson JP (standing right) April 1993–April 1995
Brian Barton (standing left) April 1995–April 1999
Graham Bober (seated centre) April 1999

PRESENT DAY BOARD OF DIRECTORS AND MANAGEMENT EXECUTIVE

ELECTED DIRECTORS

Graham Bober   President of the Society
Director since 1981
Member of Co-operative Union Central Executive
Southern Sectional Board and Education Executive
Chairman of the Pension Fund Trustees
Honorary Alderman of Colchester

Vice President of the Society   Ken Cooke
Director since 1977
Pension Fund Trustee
Honorary Alderman of Colchester

Gillian Bober   Director since 1977
Chairman of Member Relations Committee
Pension Fund Trustee
Chair of Co-operative Union Education Executive
Board of Management – Co-op College

Director since 1993   Colin Barrett
Member Relations Committee Member
Pension Fund Trustee

Sara Green   Director since 1995
Director of East Anglia Federal Co-operative Society

Director since 1995 Dianne Dallender-Jones

Sylvia Overnell   Director since 1996
Pension Fund Trustee

Director since 1996   M. Winifred Barritt
Member Relations Committee Member
Pension Fund Trustee

Jackie Bowis   Director since 1999
First employee elected to Board

Director since 1999   Roger Smith

Tony Constable   Director since 1999
Director of East Anglia Federal Co-operative Society

MANAGEMENT EXECUTIVE

Chris Blanchett
Chief Executive
Officer

Chris Orchard
Financial Controller

Colin Martin
General Manager
– Food

Peter Johnstone
General Manager
– Non-Food

Terry Mays
General Manager –
Personnel Services

James Day
Society Secretary
and Legal Officer

INDEX

Numbers in **bold** refer to illustrations

Abbot's Road 64
Allied shop **33**, 40
Automated Teller Machine 54

Barker, Don 38
Barton, Brian 61, **70**
Blanchett, Chris 54, 56, 57, 58, 59, 60, 69
Board of Directors 37, 40, 44, 45, 55, 56, 59, 61, **71**
Board, executive 37
Board of Management 14
Bober, Gillian **61**
Bober, Graham 71, **70**
Bowis, Jackie **61**
Brightlingsea 14, 16, 42, 52, 56, 66
Burnham-on-Crouch 42, 52

Castle, John **7**, 8, 9, 10, 13
Chelmsford 51
Clacton Society 21
Clacton-on-Sea 21, 23, 36, 42, 52, 54, 63
Coggeshall 23
Colchester and East Essex Co-operative and Industrial Society 7, 9
Colchester Castle **7**
Committee of Management 26, 30, 32, 35, 36, 37, 55
Co-op Fiveways 42, 51
Co-operative Bank 54, 56, 59, 66
Co-operative Day 28, **45**, **52**, **54**
Co-operative Independent Commission 32
Co-operative Insurance Society 16, 30
Co-operative movement 18, 22, 32
Co-operative societies 8, 32, 34
Co-operative Union 32
Co-operative Wholesale Society (CWS) **10**, 12, 19, 33, **51**, 54, 66
Culver Street **9**, 10, 13, **13**, **48**

Dallender, Dennis 21, 28, 30, 36, 37, 44, 45, 49, 51, **70**
Dand, Mr 7
Day, James **61**
Dedham 23, **22–3**
Dividend 9, 17, 29, 32, 36, 41, 48, **58**, 59
Dividend stamp 38, 41, 42, 44, 51, 53, **58**, **59**, 60
Dividend swipe card **59**, 60
Dovercourt **14**, **41**, 42, 54, 63

Earl's Colne 41
Education Committee 10, 14, 24, 26, **28**, 28, 36, 37
Electronix store **52**, 53, 54, 64

Fisher, H.H. 29, 30
Fiveways 42, **44**, 48, 52, 53, 54, 56, 58, 61, 63, **63**, 64
Frinton-on-Sea 36, 42, 54

Hallmark, Norman 35
Harwich **38**, **39**
Harwich, Dovercourt and Parkeston Co-operative Society 22, **24**, 38
Holland-on-Sea 22, 44
Homemaker store 52, **62**, 64
Humm, Fred 26

Ipswich 51, 53
Ipswich and Norwich Co-operative Society 59

Lexden 14, 23
Long Wyre Street **9**, **10**, 12, **13**, 14, 20, 22, **28**, **29**, 31, 40, 47, 52, **66**, 66

Maldon 40, **45**
Manningtree 14, 16, 23, **30-1**, 42, 56
Manningtree Co-operative Society **12**

Member Relations 42, 37, 57, 66
Member Relations Committee **61**
Mersea 17, **46-7**, 54, **65**
Mistley **14**
Munson, Donald 28, 57, 61, **71**

Old Heath 22
Owen, J.E.D. (Jack) 35

Pope, F.A. 25
Porter, Councillor 35
Public Relations 66

Ramsey **34**
Rochdale Society 8
Round, Derek 45, 46, 49, 52, 54, 56
Rowhedge 14, 40

St Nicholas Church 10,
St Nicholas House 29, 30, 31, 42, 65
St Nicholas site **26**
shares 48
Smith, Basil 28, 37, 45, 51, **52**, 57, **71**

The Wheatsheaf 17, 20
Tiptree 17, 36, 40, **40**, 42, **60**
Tollesbury 22, 23, 51
Transport Committee 20
Trinity Street **35**

Upper Dovercourt 44

Victoria Place 20, 26, **28**, 30, 36, 61, 65

Walton-on-the-Naze 23, 31, 40
West Mersea 23, 42, **46**, **65**
Williams, Frank 41
Witham **18**, **19**, 40, 42, 44, 54, 63
Wivenhoe 14, 23, **26**, 44
Wyre Street 13, 16, 19, 31